Things People Do for Fun

Written by Peter and Sheryl Sloan

Some people like to skydive.
They jump out of planes.
They fall through the air.
They are called skydivers.

These people are surfers.
They ride waves on surfboards.
They surf through the waves.

These people like riding.
They are called rodeo riders.
They ride bucking broncos.
Sometimes, the horses buck them off.

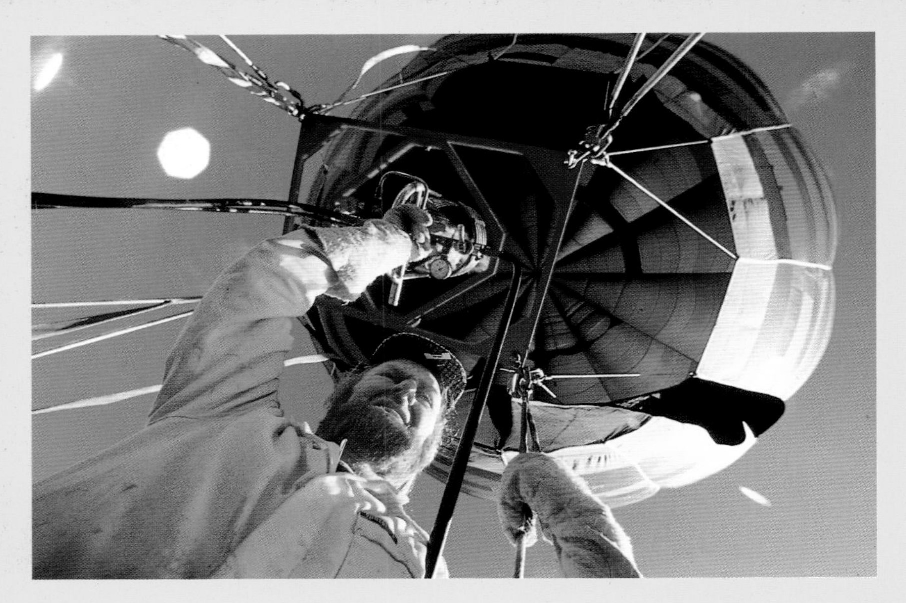

These people are called balloonists.
They use hot-air balloons.
Some people have fun floating in the sky.

These people go hang gliding.
They fly on hang gliders.
They have fun as they glide in the sky.

These people are trail bike riders.
They ride trail bikes.
They have fun
bouncing over bumpy trails.

These people are divers.
They dive down into the sea.
Sometimes, they catch fish.
Sometimes, they see sharks!

Computer